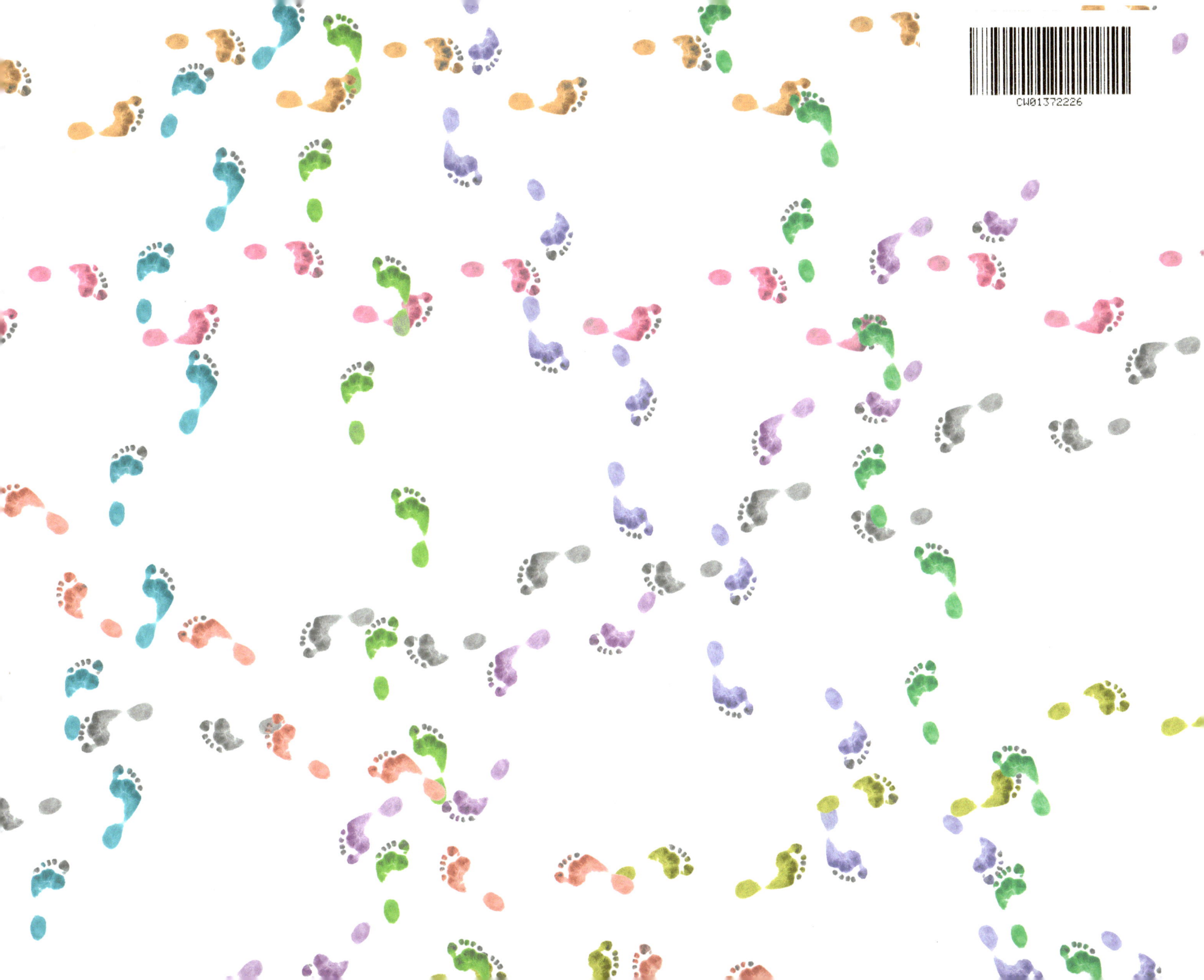

FOR INDIE,
STAY CURIOUS
KEEP SMILING,
IT'S THE LITTLE THINGS.

Feel calm and centred with a guided meditation
for grounding by author H. J. Ray.
Visit www.mywellbeingschool.com/mybarefeet

Published by My Wellbeing School 2020
Text and illustrations copyright H. J. Ray
ISBN: 978-0-6488455-2-2

Oh look it's a bee!

...BBBBZZZZZZZZZZZZZZ...

Thank you little bee for all your hard work.

...O...EI...OW...OWWWWW

Naughty little crab.

No! I am not your breakfast!

Have you ever walked barefoot through the leaves?

...CRUNCH, CRACKLE, SWOOSH...

I like to throw the leaves high up into the sky and watch them float down around me.

Have you ever walked barefoot through the mud?

...EEEEEEE||||||...

The sticky, oozy mud slips around my feet,

it sounds all squelchy and sloppy.

...SQUELCH, SLOP, SQUISH...

I just love the way it feels.

Have you ever walked barefoot through the water?

...SPLISH, SPLASH, SPLOOSH...

So fresh, cool and flowy.

My feet are all clean again.

When I stand very still,

I CAN SEE MY REFLECTION.

Have you ever walked barefoot through the snow?

...BRRRRRRRRRR...

The cold snow freezes my toes until I can't feel them.

But the white snow makes the world feel perfect.

Have you ever walked barefoot through the streets?

It's cold and hard and makes my feet ache.

I prefer the GRASS

or the WATER,

or even the SNOW!

...AAAAHHHHH... fluffy warm slippers,

I like this feeling!

...SOFT, COZY AND SNUGGLY...

My feet are all warm again.

WHAT IS YOUR FAVOURITE FEELING?

FREEZING

FRESH

SNUGGLY   HARD

I love exploring the world with

MY

BARE

FEET

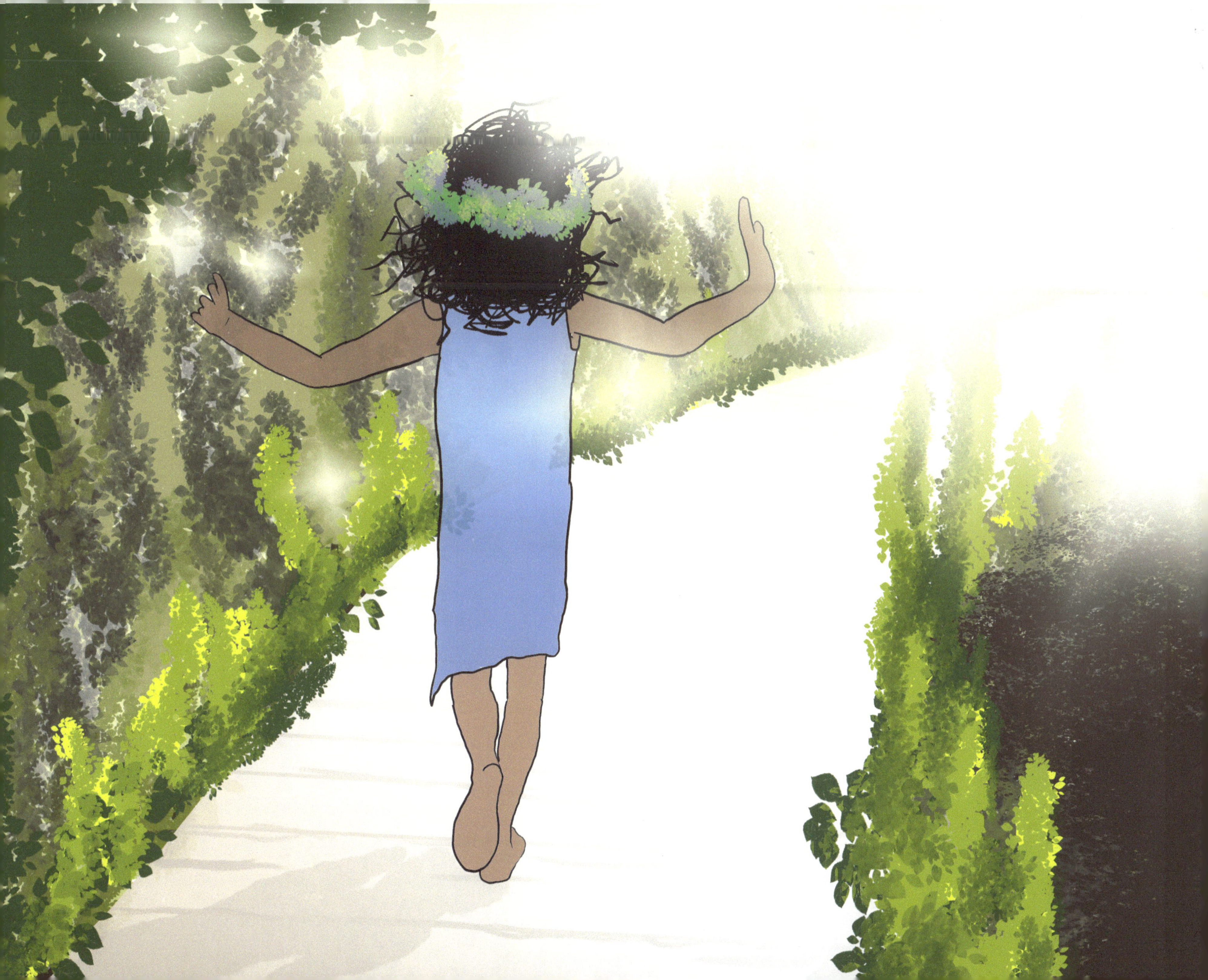

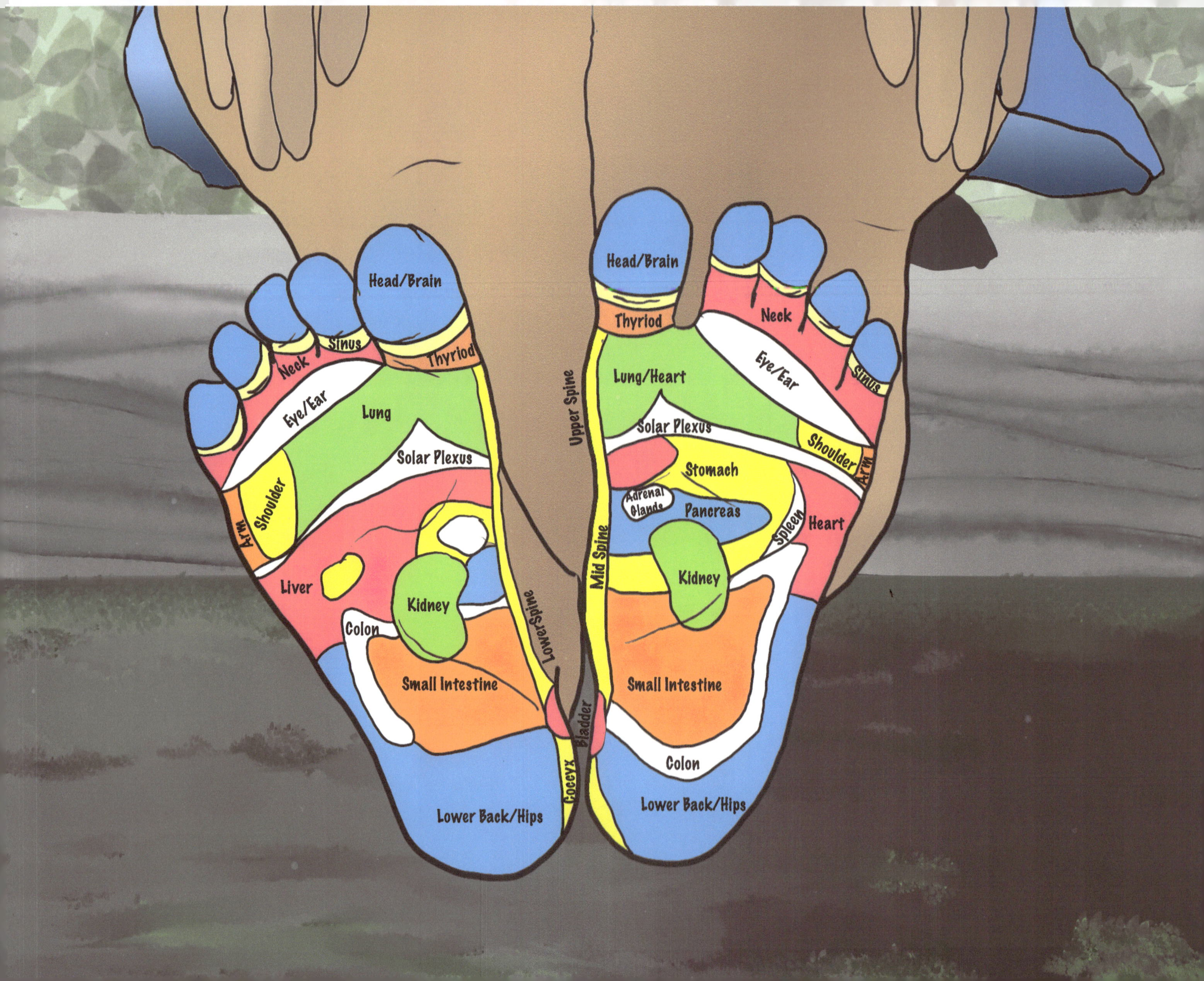
Head/Brain
Sinus
Neck
Thyriod
Eye/Ear
Lung
Solar Plexus
Shoulder
Arm
Liver
Kidney
Colon
Small Intestine
Lower Spine
Coccyx
Lower Back/Hips
Upper Spine
Mid Spine
Bladder
Head/Brain
Thyriod
Neck
Eye/Ear
Sinus
Lung/Heart
Solar Plexus
Shoulder
Arm
Stomach
Adrenal Glands
Pancreas
Spleen
Heart
Kidney
Small Intestine
Colon
Lower Back/Hips

Did you know that your feet connect to every part of your body?
So walking barefoot is actually really good for you!

THIS IS A REFLEXOLOGY CHART.

Walking with your bare feet can help you to feel calm and connected to the earth, this is called GROUNDING.

When you walk barefoot, you allow every part of your foot to move properly, which boosts the health of your entire body.

OUR FEET ARE AMAZING!

Give someone you love a FOOT MASSAGE by rubbing your hands in soft circles on different parts of their feet. Use the chart opposite to see which part of their body you are touching.

Keep your eyes open when you walk barefoot, so you don't walk on anything sharp.

HAPPY WALKING.

MY BARE FEET
Guided Meditation

www.mywellbeingschool.com/mybarefeet

I hope you enjoyed this story.

I have included a few learning resources in the book, also available on www.mywellbeingschool.com/mybarefeet to help you continue to explore the ideas in the story with your child. I am a huge believer in dialogue and would love to connect with you to continue the important conversation around mental, emotional and physical wellbeing.

HAVE YOU TRIED THE GUIDED MEDITATION YET?
I recorded a special guided meditation based on this story. I invite you to try it with your family. It is a conscious walking meditation, ideally practised outside to explore grounding and mindfulness to help your young person feel balanced and calm.

I am also an immense journalling advocate and encourage readers to take time to reflect on the story. My journal pages are also available to download on the website, or you can ask your young person to use the journal page in this book. These pages were designed to help your young person reflect on their thoughts and feelings in a non-linear, creative format.

A FEW TIPS ON HOW TO USE THE JOURNAL PAGE:
- ✓ There is no right or wrong answer.
- ✓ Doodle, sketch, draw or write your feelings.
- ✓ Don't worry about spelling.
- ✓ Guide your young person to journal mindfully.

Take a photo of your self-reflection page and tag @MYWELLBEINGSCHOOL on Instagram.

I look forward to connecting with you in the future,

With love and gratitude,

HJRay

www.mywellbeingschool.com/mybarefeet

What did this story make you think about?

How did this story make you feel?

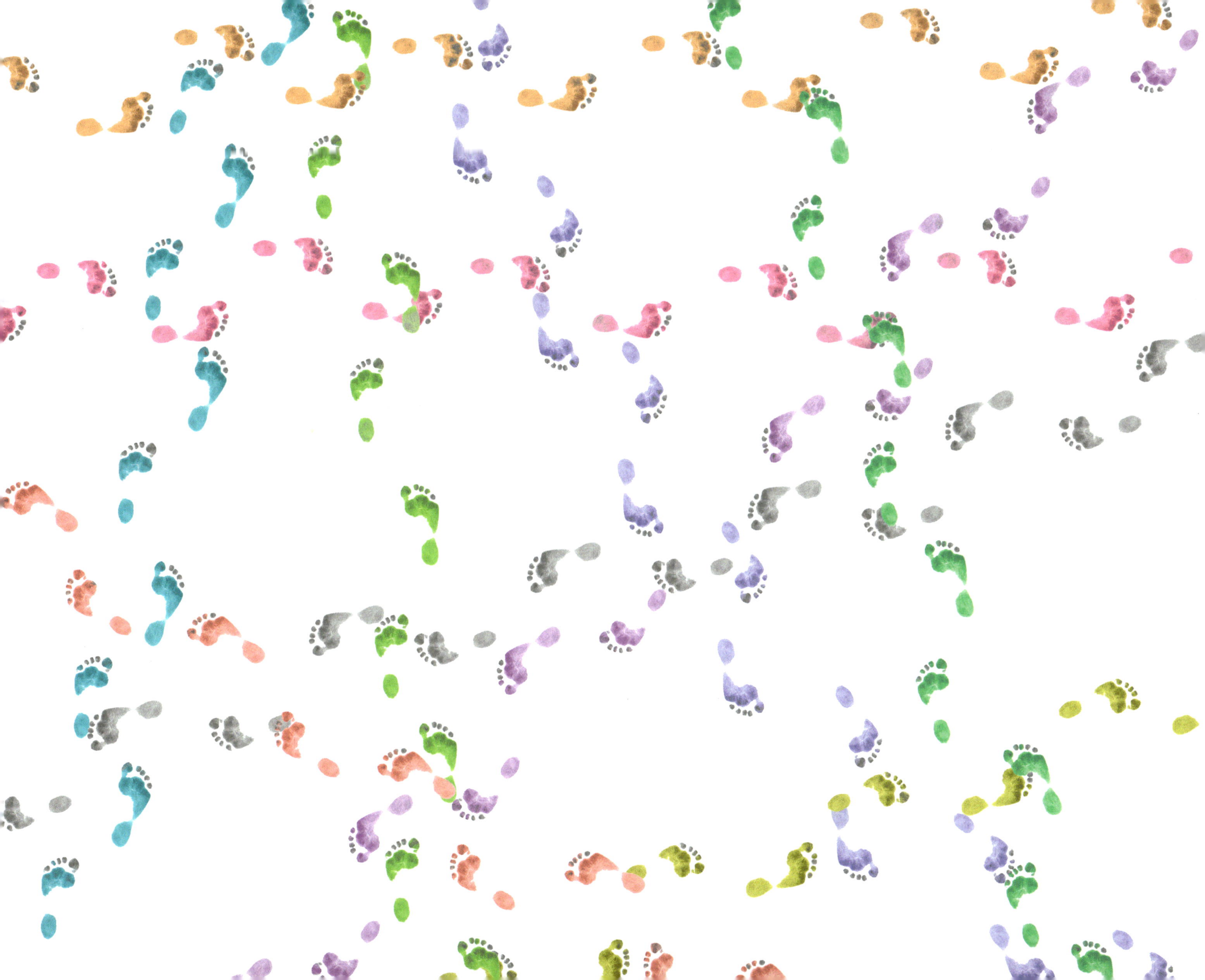

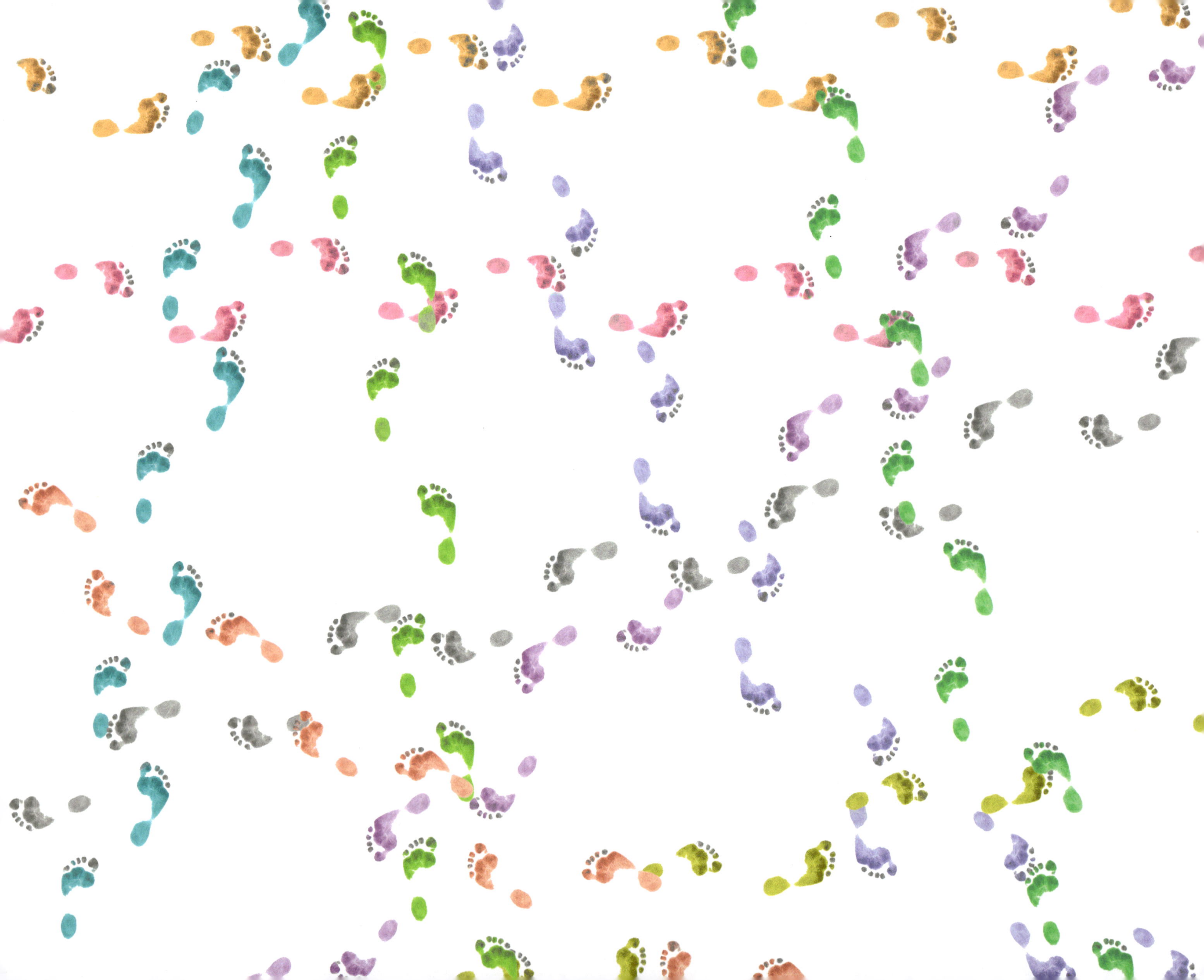

CPSIA information can be obtained
at www.ICGtesting.com
Printed in the USA
LVHW011938300123
738244LV00003B/31